TROLLS

VS.

FAIRIES

Disclaimer:

The creatures in this book are not real. They are from myths. They are fun to imagine. Read the 45th Parallel Press series Magic, Myth, and Mystery to learn more about them.

45TH PARALLEL PRESS

Published in the United States of America by Cherry Lake Publishing
Ann Arbor, Michigan
www.cherrylakepublishing.com

Reading Adviser: Marla Conn, MS, Ed., Literacy specialist, Read-Ability Inc.
Book Designer: Melinda Millward

Photo Credits: © DM7/Shutterstock.com, back cover, cover, 5, 10; © Irina Alexandrovna/Shutterstock.com, cover, 5; © Joe Therasakdhi/Shutterstock.com, cover, 5; © Digital Storm/Shutterstock.com, 6, 9; © Joost van Uffelen/Shutterstock.com, 9; © Atelier Sommerland/Shutterstock.com, 12, 15; © tsuneomp/Shutterstock.com, 16; © mel-nik/istockphoto.com, 19; © GraphicsRF/Shutterstock.com, 19, 20; © vectortatu/Shutterstock.com, 20; © AntonKarlik/Shutterstock.com, 21; © NicolasMcComber/istockphoto.com, 23; © shaineast/Shutterstock.com, 24; © Heath Johnson/Shutterstock.com, 25; © Linda Nguyen from Austin/Shutterstock.com, 25; © A Stock-Studio/Shutterstock.com, 27; © Wisconsinart/Dreamstime.com, 29

Graphic Element Credits: © studiostoks/Shutterstock.com, back cover, multiple interior pages; © infostocker/Shutterstock.com, back cover, multiple interior pages; © mxbfilms/Shutterstock.com, front cover; © MF production/Shutterstock.com, front cover, multiple interior pages; © AldanNi/Shutterstock.com, front cover, multiple interior pages; © Andrii Symonenko/Shutterstock.com, front cover, multiple interior pages; © acidmit/Shutterstock.com, front cover, multiple interior pages; © manop/Shutterstock.com, multiple interior pages; © Lina Kalina/Shutterstock.com, multiple interior pages; © mejorana/Shutterstock.com, multiple interior pages; © NoraVector/Shutterstock.com, multiple interior pages; © Smirnov Viacheslav/Shutterstock.com, multiple interior pages; © Piotr Urakau/Shutterstock.com, multiple interior pages; © IMOGI graphics/Shutterstock.com, multiple interior pages; © jirawat phueksriphan/Shutterstock.com, multiple interior pages

45th Parallel Press is an imprint of Cherry Lake Publishing.

Library of Congress Cataloging-in-Publication Data

Names: Loh-Hagan, Virginia, author.
Title: Trolls vs. fairies / by Virginia Loh-Hagan.
Other titles: Trolls versus fairies
Description: Ann Arbor, Michigan : Cherry Lake Publishing, 2020. | Series: Battle royale : lethal warriors | Includes index.
Identifiers: LCCN 2019032979 (print) | LCCN 2019032980 (ebook) | ISBN 9781534159365 (hardcover) | ISBN 9781534161665 (paperback) | ISBN 9781534160514 (pdf) | ISBN 9781534162815 (ebook)
Subjects: LCSH: Trolls—Juvenile literature. | Fairies—Juvenile literature.
Classification: LCC GR555 .L653 2020 (print) | LCC GR555 (ebook) | DDC 398.21—dc23
LC record available at https://lccn.loc.gov/2019032979
LC ebook record available at https://lccn.loc.gov/2019032980

Printed in the United States of America
Corporate Graphics

About the Author

Dr. Virginia Loh-Hagan is an author, university professor, and former classroom teacher. She believes in fairies. She lives in San Diego with her very tall husband and very naughty dogs. To learn more about her, visit www.virginialoh.com.

Table of Contents

3

Introduction

Imagine a battle between trolls and fairies. Who would win? Who would lose?

Enter the world of *Battle Royale: Lethal* **Warriors**! Warriors are fighters. This is a fight to the death! The last team standing is the **victor**! Victors are winners. They get to live.

Opponents are fighters who compete against each other. They challenge each other. They fight with everything they've got. They use weapons. They use their special skills. They use their powers.

They're not fighting for prizes. They're not fighting for honor. They're fighting for their lives. Victory is their only option.

Let the games begin!

VS.

TROLLS

Troll is an old Norse word. It means "someone who walks clumsily."

Trolls are monsters. They have **trolleri**. Trolleri is troll magic. It's dangerous and powerful. It's intended to harm others. Trolls use trolleri to control humans' minds. They control humans' hearts. They control nature. They make thick fog. They resist other monsters' magic. They change into animals. They change into humans.

Trolls are **solitary**. They're loners. They're not really social. They don't talk much. But they do live in small **packs**. Packs are groups. They follow a leader. Each pack has a king and queen. They hunt together. They attack together. They're active at night. They rest during the day. They're violent fighters. They throw large stones. They use clubs. They use tree trunks. They smash. They crush.

Some trolls are giants. They smell really bad. They're hairy. They have long noses. They have large feet. They have large hands. They have jutting jaws. Their foreheads stick out. They have tough skin. They may have tusks. Some only have 1 eye. Some have several heads. Some have tails.

Some trolls are small. They have stubby arms and legs. They have fat stomachs. They have tangled hair.

Some trolls look like humans. They're called **huldrefolk**. This means "hidden folk." They're beautiful. They have long cow tails. They charm humans and turn them into slaves. If they marry humans, they can become humans. But they lose their beauty. They're known as troll-wives.

One story features a really huge troll. The troll fishes for whales. He eats whales for dinner.

Trolls are great thieves. They steal food. They kidnap humans. They steal gold and gems. They protect their treasures.

They live for thousands of years. Nothing pierces their skin. Only magical weapons can get through their skin. They heal quickly. Trolls can **regenerate**. They regrow missing body parts. If they're really hungry, they eat their own body parts. They just grow new ones.

Sunlight is the only way to stop a troll. Sunlight turns trolls into stone. Sometimes, it makes trolls explode. This is why trolls are afraid of light. Being dumb is also their weakness. Trolls can be tricked very easily.

FUN FACTS ABOUT TROLLS

- Senja is an island in Norway. It has the world's largest troll. It's called the Senja Troll. It's about 60 feet (18 meters) tall. It weighs 275,000 pounds (124,738 kilograms). There's a family park inside. Visitors can walk through the troll's guts.

- Troll Peaks are huge mountains. They're in central Norway. People believe they're the remains of dead trolls.

- Troll stories started in Norway. They started in the early ninth century. Bragi Boddason was a Viking poet. Vikings were Norse warriors. He traveled. He told stories. He entertained kings and queens. He met a female troll. This was his most famous story. This was the first story about trolls. Boddason and the troll had a poem contest. The troll described herself. Boddason told a better poem. The troll let him escape.

- Some people believe trolls come from Neanderthals. Neanderthals were a type of human species. They no longer exist. Trolls may be the last remaining Neanderthals. Their faces are similar.

FAIRIES

Other types of fairies include leprechauns, goblins, and even trolls.

Fairies are magical creatures. They're **supernatural**. They're beyond the laws of nature. They control fate. They used to live with humans. This was when humans believed in magic. Then, humans stopped believing in magic. So, fairies hid. But they're still here. They live all around us. They make themselves invisible. They appear. They disappear. They do this quickly. They feel weak when seen by humans.

Fairies can look human. But they're not. Some are way smaller. Some are the same size. Some are giants. Some have wings. Some are beautiful. Some are ugly. There are many different types of fairies.

All fairies have magical powers. Some fairies practice **dark magic**. This is bad magic. Some fairies practice **light magic**. This is good magic. Fairies can be good. They can be bad.

Fairies interact with humans in different ways. They test humans. They change into beggars. They see if humans will help them. They reward helpful humans. They punish unhelpful humans. They play **pranks** on humans. Pranks are tricks. They tangle humans' hair. They steal their belongings. Some pranks are harmless. Some pranks are dangerous.

Fairies get humans in their debt. They help humans. Then, humans have to repay them. Humans and fairies are bonded. Once this happens, fairies are hard to get rid of.

Fairies are born from elements. Elements are earth, water, air, and fire.

Some humans try to capture fairies. They want fairy treasures. Fairies don't like to be tricked. They'll get even. Fairies trick humans. They give them **nectar**. Nectar is like a honey drink. Once humans drink, they can never escape.

Fairies can be dangerous. Some fairies are like vampires. They hunt humans. They drink humans' blood. They kidnap humans.

They can change into animals. They can talk to animals. They create **illusions**. Illusions are when things look like things they're not. They move quickly. They have super senses. They can fly.

FUN FACTS ABOUT FAIRIES

- Some people in Ireland built fairy paths in their houses. They built their front and back doors directly opposite each other. They left doors open. This allowed fairies to travel through the house.

- Fairies have a lot of power on Halloween night. Some parents in Northern Ireland were afraid fairies would kidnap their children. They put oatmeal and salt in their children's hair. This warded off fairies.

- Ly Erg is a Scottish fairy. He's small. He's dressed like a soldier. He has a red hand. The red is blood. When people fight him, they die in 2 weeks.

- Muryans were Cornish fairies. They had bad souls. They used to be humans. They did bad deeds. They got smaller and smaller. They became the size of ants. This is why Cornish people think it is bad luck to attack anthills.

- Will-o'-the-wisps are balls of light. They're seen over swamps. Some people think they're dancing fairies.

CHOOSE YOUR BATTLEGROUND

Trolls and fairies are fierce fighters. They're well-matched. They both have similar powers. They're magical. They're tricky. But they have different ways of fighting. They also have different weaknesses. So, choose your battleground carefully!

Battleground #1: Sea

- Trolls are from Norway. Norway is on the water. There are a lot of fishermen. Trolls are used to the sea, but they prefer land.

- Fairies like to be around water. Most fairies are tiny. So, they can get around very easily. They disguise themselves as twinkling lights in water.

Fairies were thought to be the stars in the night sky.

Battleground #2: Land

- Trolls would be well hidden on land. They are part of nature. They blend in. Plants and trees grow on them.

  - Fairies also hide well on land. They are found where humans are. They live in houses. They like to blend in with city lights.

Battleground #3: Mountains

- Trolls would happily fight in mountains. Large mountain trolls are big. They look like rocks when sleeping. They have soil on their neck and shoulders. Pine trees grow from the soil. They live far away from humans.

  - Fairies would be fine fighting in the mountains. They can fly.

ARMED AND DANGEROUS: WEAPONS

Trolls: Trolls like to use battle-axes. These axes are made for war. They have long handles. They have sharp blades at the end. They're light. They're fast. Trolls swing these axes. They can also throw them. Some axes have a lower blade. They can be used to pull down opponents' shields. Some axes are so heavy that it takes 2 trolls to hold them.

Fairies: Fairies' best weapon is fairy dust. It's also known as pixie dust. Fairy dust looks like glitter. It's magic. Fairies sprinkle it around. They say spells. Spells have magical powers. The fairy dust makes the magic happen. Fairy dust can do all kinds of things. It can give the power to fly. It can help make plants grow. It can heal wounds. Different colors of fairy dust do different things. Fairy dust that is left behind forms a fairy ring. Fairy rings are circles of mushrooms.

FIGHT ON!

The battle begins! It's nighttime. Trolls and fairies can both see in the dark. They're on a mountaintop. There are a lot of trees. There are a lot of plants.

Move 1:

Fairies fly around. They look like fireflies. They're looking for trolls. They look closely at all the rocks. They won't be fooled. They know trolls like to pretend to be rocks. The fairies sniff the air. They try to pick up the trolls' scent. They look for troll tracks on the ground. They look for bits of crushed rocks. They look for cracks in the ground.

Fairies live among humans. But they don't like to be seen.

Move 2:

Trolls see the fairies. They slowly get up. The earth quakes a little. Trolls gather iron from the earth. They make iron cages. They want to trap fairies inside. This will stop fairy magic. Fairies don't like iron. If fairies touch iron, they can die. Iron makes them back off. To fairies, iron feels like walking on broken glass. To them, iron smells like rotten eggs.

Move 3:

Fairies want to distract trolls from making iron cages. They sprinkle some fairy dust. They say a spell. The fairies create the sound of church bells. They know trolls hate church bells.

Even dragons respect trolls' powers.

LIFE SOURCE: FOOD FOR BATTLE

Trolls: Trolls eat anything. They're not picky eaters. They eat rocks. They eat trees. They eat humans. They eat livestock. Livestock means farm animals. Examples are goats, cows, and pigs. Trolls eat things whole. So, they'll eat bones too. They have very strong stomachs. The stomachs break down anything they eat. Some trolls use their vomit as weapons. They'll vomit on their opponents. Vomit means to throw up.

Fairies: Fairies love sweet food. They love all types of desserts. They love cake. They love ice cream. They love candy. They love sweet butter. They love honey. They love fresh, creamy milk. Sometimes, people leave food outside of kitchens. Fairies will eat this food. They're known for taking bites of pies left to cool. They eat tiny bites so people won't notice.

Move 4:

The church bells upset the trolls. The trolls stop working. They throw big rocks at the sounds. They think they're throwing rocks at churches. Trolls' breath has power. Their breath spoils everything. They breathe on the fairies.

Move 5:

Fairies sprinkle dust and say a spell. They make a shield. They keep the rocks away. They keep the trolls' breath away.

Move 6:

Trolls march toward the fairies.

Move 7:

Fairies circle around the trolls. They make a fairy ring. They want to lure trolls in the middle. If they do, the magic will force the trolls to dance forever. The trolls would die from being too tired.

Pixies are another type of fairy.
They often wear green.

AND THE VICTOR IS . . .

What are their next moves?
Who do you think would win?

Trolls could win if:

- They don't accept any gifts or favors from fairies. Fairies will want something in return. Dealing with fairy magic is dangerous.
- They don't drink or eat anything from the fairy world. If they do, they'll be stuck in the fairy world. Fairies will steal years from their lives.

Fairies could win if:

- They confuse trolls. They can tell jokes. They can tell riddles. Trolls are not smart. They don't like to think.
- They distract the trolls until sunrise. The sun will make the trolls turn to stone.

Fairies and trolls have served many gods and goddesses.

Trolls: Top Champion

Jotunn were **Norse** giants. They were from the area around Norway. In some stories, the jotunn and trolls were the same creatures. Sinmara was a jotunn. She was the wife of Surt. Surt was the king of the fire giants. That made Sinmara the queen of fire giants. She lived in Muspelheim. Muspelheim was the land of fire. Sinmara's name meant "nervous nightmare." Her job was to guard Laevateinn. Laevateinn was a dangerous weapon. It meant "wounding wand." It was a powerful stick. It was from the doors of death. Sinmara kept Laevateinn in a box. The box had 9 locks. Sinmara could only give the weapon to a special hero. The hero had to bring her Vioopnir's feather. Vioopnir was a glittering golden rooster. The hero had to get a feather. He had to put it in a bag. He had to bring the bag to Sinmara. But this task was impossible. The hero needed Laevateinn to get the feather.